P9-DNW-751

THE **FORTIES** IN PICTURES

James Lescott

THE **FORTIES** IN PICTURES

PaRragon

Bath · New York · Singapore · Hong Kong · Cologne · Delhi · Melbourne

This is a Parragon Book
First published in 2007

Parragon Books Ltd
Queen Street House
4 Queen Street
Bath, BA1 1HE

Created and produced by:
Endeavour London Ltd.
21-31 Woodfield Road
London W9 2BA

With great thanks to the team
at Endeavour London Ltd. –
Jennifer Jeffrey, Kate Pink,
Franziska Payer-Crockett and
Liz Ihre

Text © Parragon Books Ltd
2007

ISBN 978-1-4054-9529-5

Printed in China

All rights reserved.
No part of this publication
may be reproduced or
transmitted in any form or by
any means, electronic or
mechanical, including
photocopying, recording, or
any information storage and
retrieval system, without
permission in writing from the
copyright holders.

All images courtesy of Getty
Images who is grateful to the
following photographers and
image libraries represented by
Getty Images for their kind
assistance.

20th Century Fox: 36; Agence
France Presse: 68, 203, 213,
228, 238(t), 239; British Lion
Films: 255; Columbia Films:
77; DisCina: 184; Frank Driggs
Collection: 75; Lambert: 161;
Library of Congress: 55(r);
MGM: 252; National Archives:
88-89, 141; National Baseball
Hall of Fame Library/MLB:
206; New York Times : 224(t),
RDA: 123, 226; RKO: 56; Roger
Viollet Collection: 118, 224(b),
225; Slava Katamidze
Collection: 49, 81, 82, 85;
Time & Life Pictures: cover, 19,
29, 42, 52, 55, 62-63, 66-67,
72-73, 76, 86, 91, 94-95, 97,
99, 100-101, 103-105, 108-109,
112-114, 122, 126-128, 131,
133, 135, 137-140, 146-147,
149, 152, 153(b), 155-156, 158,
160, 164, 169, 171-173, 182,
187-188, 190(b), 198-202, 212,
216, 227, 229-231, 240-241,
250, 252-253; US Airforce: 93;
US Army: 92; United Artists:
37, 132; US Marine Corps:157;
Universal Pictures: 185;
Warner Bros: 57

Frontispiece

With the war in Europe over, fashion raised its
beautiful head, and hemlines. Three British
models stride out to show off their *chic*, which
was strictly for export only, July 21, 1945.

Page 7

US forces display their strength at an air display
over the *USS Missouri* on VJ Day, September 2,
1945. A few hours earlier, the Japanese had
signed their surrender on board the battleship.

Contents

Introduction

In 1940 the air defence of parts of Britain was still entrusted to squadrons of biplanes and some men rode to war on horseback. By 1949 a young American pilot had become the first man to break the sound barrier, and the automobile was about to enter its first golden era. Those lucky enough to live through the 1940's saw old ways of life disappear at the tear away speed that war always generates. They saw destruction on an unprecedented scale, cruelty almost beyond imagination, and progress that took the breath away. New nations appeared, old empires crumbled, and the world divided itself into two great power blocs. To the east was Communism – grim and defensive. To the west was Capitalism – glamorous and aggressive. And hanging over the entire planet was the menace of the A-bomb.

It was a time that produced all that is best and worst in the human species – heroism and barbarity, self-sacrifice and greed, noble endeavor and brute treachery. Nobody knows how many people died in World War II, but estimates vary between 50 and 60 million. The majority of the victims died in Europe or Asia, but the scythe of Death also managed to cut down many in Africa and Australasia, and was ready and waiting for the young warriors of the United States and Canada when they hurried across the Atlantic to "do their bit".

When it was over, chaos was quickly swept away. There was a new attempt at establishing a world forum that could deal with disease, poverty, famine, and intra-national quarrels. The United Nations was born in San Francisco but settled in New York. In the preamble to its Charter, issued on October 24, 1945, it proclaimed its aims, among them "To reaffirm faith in fundamental human rights, in the dignity and worth of the human person, in the equal rights of men and women and of nations large and small…"

Out of the smoke and fury of a dreadful war had come clarity and undeniably common sense. It was a bold end to a fearsome decade.

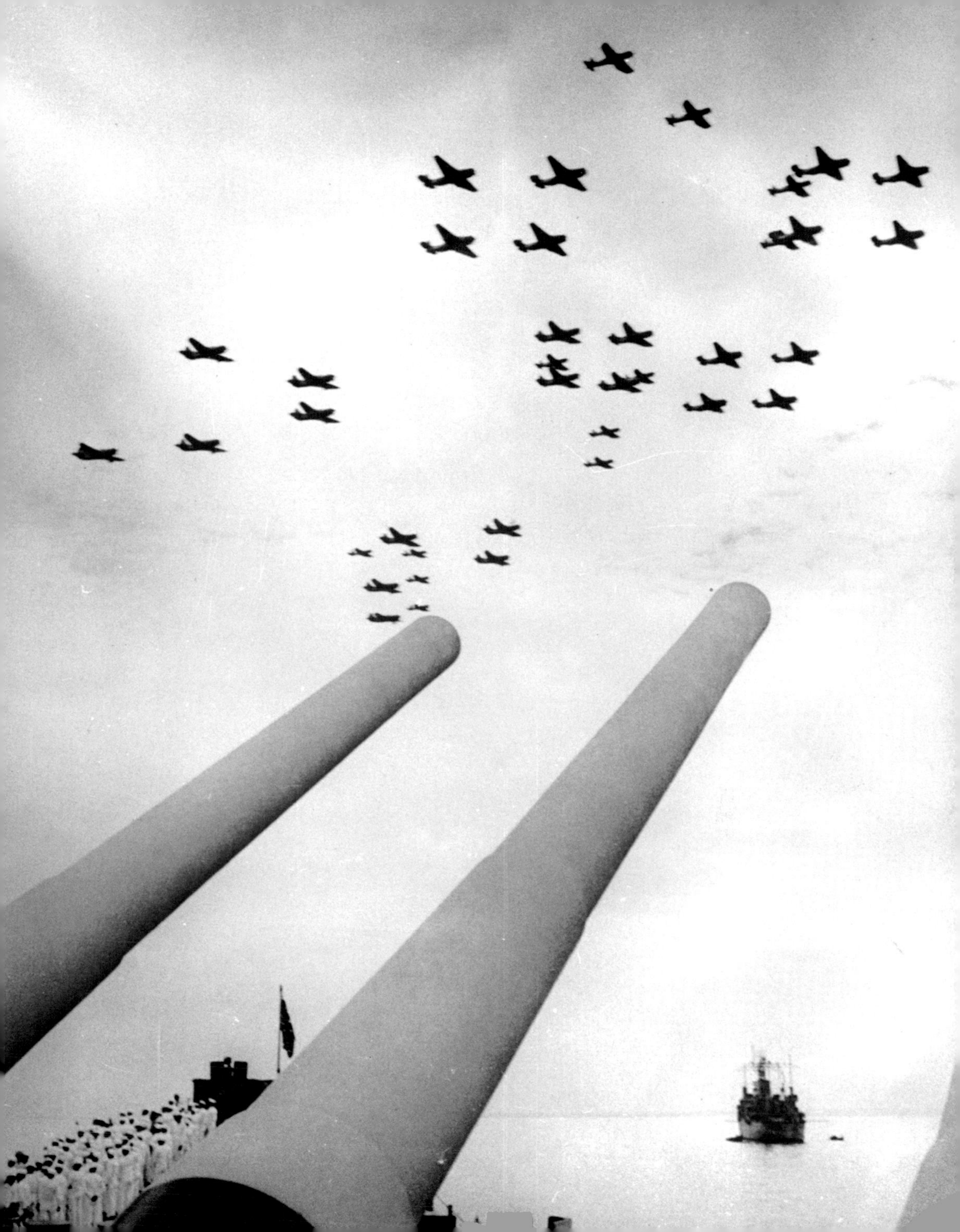

The war was nine months old. After a period of relative inactivity, the German army launched a major offensive in May 1940, overrunning Holland in five days and driving back the French, Belgian, and British armies. When the Germans paused to rest their troops and repair their tanks, over 100,000 French soldiers and 250,000 British soldiers gathered on the beaches of **Dunkirk** (*right*), desperate for rescue.

The rescue at **Dunkirk** was delivered by ships of the French and Royal Navy, and a flotilla of "little ships", privately owned and manned by volunteers. (*Left*) British troops wade through the shallows to reach a boat. (*Right*) Members of the crew of the French destroyer *Bourrasque* are picked up by a British warship. The *Bourrasque* had struck a mine and was sinking.

Members of the
British Expeditionary
Force (*left*) gather
on deck after their
escape from the
Dunkirk beaches.
On a single day –
May 31 – 68,000
soldiers were saved.

Exhausted British soldiers, newly returned from **Dunkirk**, take a train from
the south coast of England. Most of them had spent their entire time in
France on the move, advancing and retreating. Few had fired a shot in anger.

Belgian refugees take cover
during an attack by the
Luftwaffe. For many of them,
this was not the first time in
their lives that war had driven
them from their homes.

One of the few delays experienced by the Germans in their *blitzkrieg*. A Panzer Division is held up by the **destruction of a bridge** in Belgium. It was of little significance ultimately. Brussels had already fallen, and the Belgian army was in full retreat.

In the weeks before Dunkirk,
British troops pass French refugees
fleeing from the advancing Germans
along a section of the **Routes
du Nord**. The British army was in
France for barely six months.

The **German advance** rolls on. The tactic of using tanks and armored carriers in lightning strikes across open country had been discussed by military strategists for twenty years, but the *Wehrmacht* was the first to put such tactics into effect.

German troops parade along the
Champs Elysees, Paris, following
the fall of France. They entered
the city virtually unopposed on
June 14, a mere five weeks after
the invasion of France.

Adolf Hitler enjoys his most relished triumph of the World War II – the occupation of Paris. His visit, on June 28, lasted just three hours, beginning at 05.30. He was accompanied by the architects Albert Speer and Herman Geisler, and the sculptor Arno Breker.

On July 1, 1940, the British Mediterranean Fleet fired on French ships in **Oran**, to prevent them falling into Nazi hands. Two battleships and a battlecruiser were destroyed, with considerable loss of life. (*Above*) French sailors fight fires on board one of their ships.

German Foreign Minister Joachim von Ribbentrop (center) looks on as **Hitler** and Marshal Henri-Philippe **Pétain** shake hands. Pétain had sought an armistice with Germany in June. Within a month, he was puppet leader of Vichy France.

Following the Fall of France, Britain prepared for a German invasion, extending detailed but largely optimistic programmes of civil defense. (*Above*) A member of the **Home Guard** drives a car which has been converted into a "Beaverbug" – a lightly armed tank named after Lord Beaverbrook.

The **Home Guard** of part-time "soldiers" was composed of civilians who trained in their spare time. (*Right*) A forerunner of the Home Guard, the Civicorps use broom handles for their rifle drill early in 1940.

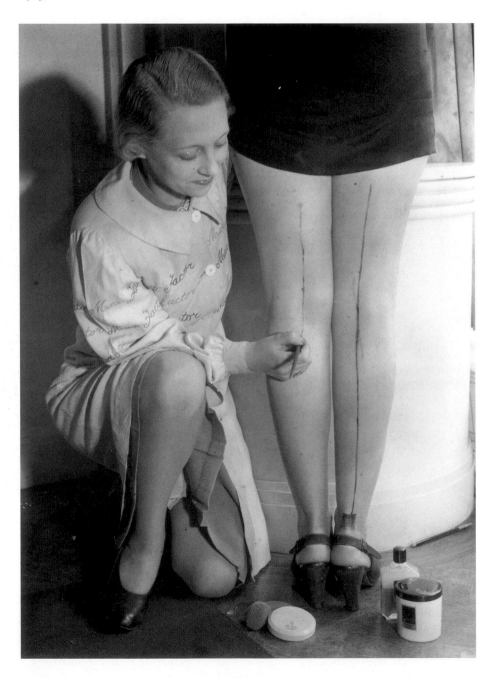

(*Above*) Shop assistants **rescue hats** and sweep broken glass from a shattered window display in the West End of London. Bomb damage to retail areas were a greater threat to civilian morale generally than raids on docks and industrial zones.

Maintaining morale in the fashion world. (*Left*) A beautician and Max Factor agent **paints a seam** on a woman's bare leg. The aim was to produce a *trompe l'œuil* effect, giving the impression that the woman was wearing the sheerest of stockings.

A child's experience of war.
(*Left*) Each one clearly labeled,
London children, who have
earlier been **evacuated** to the
South Coast, now await
transport to new reception
areas inland during the threat
of German invasion, July 14.
(*Above*) With sweets and ice
creams either rationed or
unobtainable, children tackle
the healthier, but tougher,
delights of a **carrot-on-a-stick**.

Two ways of financing the war. (*Left*) A **poster of Winston Churchill** exhorts the British to invest in a victory drive. It was designed by students at the Brighton School of Art not long after Churchill became Prime Minister in October 1940. (*Above*) London office workers gather in the street to watch a **mobile cinema unit** showing film of RAF successes. The screening was aimed at raising money for the war effort as the Battle of Britain neared its climax in October.

The **Battle of Britain** lasted from June to October 1940.
It began after the Fall of France and ended when the
Luftwaffe turned its attention to bombing London and
other major cities. (*Above*) A squadron of *Spitfires*
patrols the English coastline. (*Right*) Pilots of 610 County
of Chester Squadron take a break between sorties at
Hawkinge airfield, August 1940. One pilot wrote:
"Most of us were pretty scared all the bloody time..."

(*Above*) A bus in the **Bounds Green** area of London lies at the bottom of a bomb crater, October 27. Such eerie sights often greeted citizens emerging from shelters after a night of bombing.

(*Right*) Two *Dornier 217* bombers fly over **Silvertown** during a raid on the London Docks. After attacking airfields and military targets, the *Luftwaffe* concentrated on such targets during the autumn of 1940.

On November 14, **Coventry** became the
first city to fall victim to a new bombing
technique. The *Kampfgruppe 100* method
used a "pathfinder" force to guide bombers
to their target, which was then saturated
with bombs. The raid on Coventry lasted
10 hours, destroying the Cathedral (*left*)
and much of the city center (*above*).

"We keep a-comin'. We're the people that live. Can't lick us. We'll go on forever… because we're the people". Jane Darwell (center), with Henry Fonda (on her left), pitching a message of survival in John Ford's film of **The Grapes of Wrath**. She won an Oscar for her performance.

Charlie Chaplin delivered a more personal message in **The Great Dictator**, his first all-talking film. It was a comic indictment of Fascism, though Chaplin's political punch was softened by sentimentality and much music-hall clowning.

For the Free French, the war continued. Their leader in exile was **Charles de Gaulle** (*left*, center), here inspecting a contingent of French colonial troops who had followed him to Britain, January 24, 1941.

For the **French Resistance**, the war had just begun. (*Above*) A group of partisans studies how to maintain weapons dropped by parachute in the Haute Loire. The glamorous image may be a propaganda photo. Ahead lay a long and bitter struggle.

Months of heavy bombing reduced parts of London to wasteland. The most devastated area, described as "a surreal waste of tangled girders", was that around **St Paul's Cathedral** (*right*). (*Above*) Firefighters, their clothes soaked in water, oil, and grease, continue to fight the flames as morning comes to the flattened city, May 1941.

(*Below*) During a massive enemy
air raid, Moscow citizens shelter
in Maiakovskaia **Metro Station**.
Other underground stations in
the city were used as hospitals.

A strong sub-culture developed in
the subway stations used as
shelters during the Blitz in
London. Underground libraries,
debating societies, and education
classes were created. (*Right*) An
ENSA concert takes place at
Aldwych Station.

(*Above*) The historic three-day meeting between President Roosevelt and Winston Churchill, Prime Minister of Britain, on board *HMS Prince of Wales* in Placentia Bay, Newfoundland, August 1941. Here they drew up the **Atlantic Charter**.

(*Right*) Churchill and his Minister of Information, Brendan Bracken, inspect bomb damage to the **Houses of Parliament**, May 11. Despite the nightly destruction, Churchill was inspired by the effort required to fight the Blitz.

The war had a profound effect on the lives of women in the combatant nations. They worked the land, staffed transport systems, provided the labor for factories, and served in the Armed Forces. (*Above*) Members of the **Women's Land Army** make hay in Suffolk, England, April 26.

(*Above*) Women **munitions workers** take a break in a British shell factory. They were supplied with a daily extra ration of milk to counteract the effects of exposure to lead in the factory. At first, such work was voluntary. Later, women were conscripted by the state.

Operation **Barbarossa** was launched
on June 22, 1941. Its aim was to
knock the USSR out of the war within
weeks and to give Hitler access to
the Soviet oilfields. (*Above*) Motorized
infantry of the *Wehrmacht* make rapid
initial advances in the Ukraine.

There was, however, no swift victory for either side. Winter closed in, bringing the German advance to a standstill, and inflicting appalling hardship on civilians made homeless by the fighting. (*Above*) A group of **Russian women and children** struggle to find a place of shelter and safety.

Pearl Harbor, Hawaii, was the home base of the Pacific Fleet. In the event of the Japanese seeking to extend their military conquests in Asia and the Pacific, it was an obvious target. Some advisers had recognized this and warned of a likely attack, but when 360 Japanese planes struck without official warning on the morning of Sunday, December 7, Pearl Harbor was off-guard. The sudden strike lasted barely two hours, but in that brief time destroyed eight US battleships, 14 smaller warships, and 200 aircraft. Japanese losses were light – some 38 planes and five midget submarines.

Reaction was swift. Roosevelt described it as "a day which will live in infamy", but promised "we will gain the inevitable triumph, so help us God". The United States immediately declared war on Japan. Three days later war was declared on Germany and Italy, whom Roosevelt claimed knew of the intended attack. A crumb of considerable comfort was that most of the aircraft carriers based at Pearl Harbor were at sea that day. These ships formed the backbone of recovery and retaliation in the bitter fighting that occurred in the Pacific over the next four years.

All six of Japan's first-line aircraft carriers took part in the attack. (*Left*) Japanese pilots are briefed on a carrier deck for the raid on Pearl Harbor.

This photograph, taken from a Japanese plane, shows the early stages of the attack on Ford Island in Pearl Harbor. The plumes of water come from bombs dropped on "Battleship Row", where the most powerful US ships lay at anchor.

(*Left*) Smoke pours from the *USS West Virginia* and *USS Tennessee* as the two battleships sunk in the water. (*Above*) The destroyer *USS Shaw* explodes. (*Below*) Having dropped its bombs on the airfield at Pearl Harbor, a Japanese light bomber heads back to its carrier.

(*Left*) A seagull flies peacefully over the dry dock at Pearl Harbor a few hours after the attack. In the foreground are the remains of the destroyers *USS Downes* and *USS Cassin*. Smoke rises from the battleship *USS Pennsylvania*, hit by a 500 lb bomb. Beyond the crane is the *USS Helena*, hit by a Japanese torpedo.

(*Left*) President Roosevelt signs the declaration of war on Japan, December 8, 1951. (*Above*) An early report in the *San Francisco Chronicle* gives news of Pearl Harbor, and anticipates Roosevelt's declaration of war on Japan.

(*Above*) "Don't be too sure I'm as crooked as I'm supposed to be". Humphrey Bogart as Sam Spade in the 1941 film **The Maltese Falcon**. It was the third and best film adaption of Dashiell Hammett's novel.

(*Left*) "I'll bet you five, you're not alive if you don't know his name..." Orson Welles booms and bellows his way through **Citizen Kane**, reckoned one of the greatest films of all time. Welles and Herman J Mankiewicz won Oscars for the film's screenplay.

The war in the East began disastrously for both Britain and the United States. Singapore, lynchpin of the British Empire fell in February, and on May 6 the United States surrendered the island of **Corregidor**. (*Left*) The Stars and Stripes is hauled down on Corregidor. (*Above*) American prisoners, taken on the island, are marched away.

As the Japanese advanced, island by island in the Pacific, hundreds of GIs were captured. (*Left*) **US prisoners of war** are searched by their Japanese guards.

(*Right*) Six months into the war the first Japanese-Americans are sent to **internment camps** from their homes in Bainbridge Island, Washington State. The woman carrying the child was born in the United States. It is possible that she returned after the war, for Bainbridge had a high return rate of internees after 1945.

Two major sea battles, fought in May and June 1942, together turned the tide of war in the Pacific. (*Left*) Crew members from the sinking *USS Lexington* struggle aboard a rescue ship during the **Battle of the Coral Sea**, May 8, 1942. (*Above*) A Japanese torpedo hits the aircraft carrier *USS Yorktown* during the **Battle of Midway**, June 4. But it was the Japanese carriers that took heavier losses – four were sunk, including two that had taken part in the attack on Pearl Harbor.

"Improvised muddle brought discreditable failure" was the historian A J P Taylor's verdict on the **Dieppe Raid** of August 19. British and Canadian troops were used for a dress rehearsal of bigger raids to come. It was a disaster. (*Left*) German soldiers examine a captured Canadian Churchill tank. (*Above*) British soldiers bring back a prisoner after the raid.

The opposing commanders at El Alamein. (*Left*) Field Marshal Erwin **Rommel**, the greatest military strategist of the war. Under his command, German losses were considerably fewer in the battle, although he felt compelled to retreat to protect his supply lines. (*Above*) **Monty** – General Bernard Law Montgomery – a maverick commander who inspired enthusiasm and loyalty in his own troops.

The Battle of **El Alamein** began on October 23, 1942 and lasted 12 days. Rommel led 100,000 German and Italian troops, Montgomery commanded 150,000 Commonwealth and Allied troops. Churchill regarded the Allied victory as marking "the end of the beginning of the war…" (*Right*) A German tank surrenders on October 25 – a picture that impressed the public in Britain.

Some of the most savage fighting of the entire war took place on the Pacific islands. (*Above*) **Japanese dead** lie on Raider's Ridge, killed in the battle for Guadalcanal, September 14, 1942. (*Right*) The **bodies of American soldiers** lie on a beach in New Guinea. This was as far as the Japanese advanced, threatening Australia and Allied supply routes in the South Pacific.

(*Left*) The engine of a **B-26 Marauder** is severed from the plane after being hit by ground fire during a raid on Toulon, France.

In the autumn of 1942, the Germans occupied Vichy France. To avoid the capture of their ships, the French crews scuttled the French fleet as it lay at anchor in **Toulon** harbor (*above*) with the loss of three battleships, seven cruisers, and 12 submarines.

(*Above*) **Dame Myra Hess** gives one of her many lunchtime piano recitals at the National Gallery, London, July 18, 1942. She played to packed houses, even during air raids. Strangely, the preferred repertoire was that taken from the works of Beethoven, Mozart, and Bach. (*Right*) While Fats Waller beams down from a poster, and vocalist Joya Sherrill smiles (center, rear), **Duke Ellington** plays for servicemen and women in Hartford, Connecticut.

Dance, whether on the screen or in the dance halls, was one of the most popular entertainments throughout the war. (*Left*) Leon James and Willa Mae Ricker demonstrate the **"Lindy Hop"**, a dance that evolved in New York clubs in the 1920s but reached its peak of popularity all over the world – including Axis countries – in the 1940s. (*Above*) **Fred Astaire and Rita Hayworth** hit the roof to the music of Jerome Kern in the 1942 film *You Were Never Lovelier*.

Two of the British Forces' favorites
were **Ivy Benson** and Vera Lynn.
Benson led an all girls band throughout
the war. Although her signature was
Lady Be Good, she lost a great many
of her musicians to romance and the
American military. (*Above*) Ivy, on
clarinet, swings out at a Halloween
Dance for GIs, November 14, 1942.

Vera Lynn was "The Forces'
Sweetheart", an accomplished singer
of most popular music, although her
biggest hits were wartime sentimental
numbers such as *We'll Meet Again* and
*There'll be Bluebirds Over the White
Cliffs of Dover*. (*Above*) On behalf of the
Variety Artistes Ladies' Guild, Vera
presents a mobile canteen to the YMCA.

1942   Stalingrad

The Nazi invasion of the Soviet Union was planned as yet another lightning strike by the hitherto invincible *Wehrmacht*. Hitler launched Operation Barbarossa in June 1941 expecting early and complete success. He saw it as a test of the Reich itself. Fifteen months later, the German 6th Army under General von Paulus laid siege to Stalingrad. Stalin's own view was that the battle that followed was the critical moment in the Great Patriotic War, a test of the resolve of the Bolshevik Revolution and of the loyalty of the Soviet People. What followed was hell on earth for millions.

In November 1942 the German besiegers of Stalingrad were themselves surrounded by units of the Red Army. Newly promoted to Field Marshal, von Paulus respectfully requested permission to break off the siege and fight his way out. Hitler turned down his request. The suffering on both sides was horrendous. By December the Germans had little food, scant ammunition, inadequate clothing and no medical supplies. On January 31, 1943, von Paulus surrendered. More than 90,000 Germans had died of cold or hunger, a further 100,000 had been killed in the previous three weeks fighting. Hitler's generals never trusted him again.

(***Right***) **In the early days of the siege, German troops shell a suburb on the outskirts of Stalingrad, September 1942. (*Far right*) The statue of Lenin stands above the ruins of Stalingrad's city center.**

Opposing views of Stalingrad. (*Right*)
German tanks cover an infantry advance,
November 1942. The picture was taken by a
German war photographer and appears to be
untouched. (*Above*) Two Russian photographs
are joined to create a telling collage of Soviet
resistance and counter-attack, doubtless
to inspire further heroism. The join is made
along the line of the dead civilian's body.

(*Above*) Soviet dive bombers pound an army already on its knees, January 1943. (*Right, and far right above*) In the last days of the battle of Stalingrad, Red Army soldiers work their way through the rubble of the city, mopping up the few remaining pockets of German resistance.

(*Right*) Soviet troops march past the remains of what had been one of Stalingrad's finest department stores. Two months earlier, the building had been the HQ of Field Marshal von Paulus and his staff. The devastation of the city was such that it was reckoned some 50 to 100 mines, bombs, and shells had exploded in each square meter of ground.

On August 7, 1942 US Marines landed on the
Solomon Islands and the ferocious six-month battle
of **Guadalcanal** began. In appalling conditions, the
slaughter was immense. (*Left*) American GIs patrol
the jungle at the foot of the 500-meter (1,680-feet)
peak known as "The Grassy Knoll". (*Above*) Sick
and starving Japanese prisoners are taken down to
the beach by American troops, February 26, 1943.

In April 1943, the inhabitants of the Jewish ghetto in Warsaw rose against their Nazi oppressors. Since the first German occupation of **Warsaw** at the beginning of the war, they had smuggled weapons into the **ghetto** and laid in a store of home-made bombs, but the uprising was doomed from its start. The Germans called up reinforcements and bitter fighting, street by street, herded the Jews into an ever-decreasing area. (*Right*) Jewish civilians begin their journey to concentration camps following the uprising.

In 1941 German **U-boats** and planes of the *Luftwaffe*
had sunk 300 ships in what became known as the first
battle of the Atlantic. As the years passed, Allied shipping
losses steadily increased, but by 1943 U-boat losses
were so heavy that Admiral Doenitz recalled them to base.
(*Left*) A U-boat crew watch as an American merchant
ship sinks. (*Above*) British merchant seamen, victims of
a U-boat raid, await rescue by a US Coastguard cutter.

After success across the breadth of North
Africa, the Allies prepared to attack Sicily.
On July 10, 1943, an armada of 3,000 warships
and transport craft dropped anchor off the
Sicilian coast and the invasion began. It met
with little resistance. (*Above*) Two weeks later,
Sicilians greet Sherman tanks in **Palermo**.

Italian support for Hitler and Mussolini rapidly
declined, but German military resistance was fierce
when Allied troops crossed the Straits of Messina
to mainland **Italy** early in September. (*Above*)
Military vehicles of the 817th Engineer Aviation
Battalion hit the beach. The plane was the victim of
"friendly fire". The pilot escaped relatively unhurt.

Two images by Margaret Bourke-White of life in Italy
during the Allied advance. (*Right*) **Neapolitans** evacuate
their city to escape danger from electronically-controlled
booby traps left behind by retreating Nazi troops.
(*Above*) Two of the many children whose families made
their homes underground to shelter from Allied bombing.

As the tide of war turned, 1943 saw a flurry of conferences between leaders of the Allied Nations fighting Nazism. (*Above*) The **Cairo Conference**, December 17, 1943: (left to right) Chiang Kai Shek, Roosevelt, Churchill, and Madame Chiang Kai Shek. (*Left*) **Casablanca**, January 14, 1943, and the reconciliation between Giraud (far left) and de Gaulle (second from right).

(*Above*) **Teheran**, November 28, 1943:
(right to left) Churchill, Roosevelt, and
Stalin (shaking hands with Churchill's
daughter Sarah). Stalin and Roosevelt
here agreed plans for the invasion of
France in 1944. (*Right*) Churchill
(seated, far right), Anthony Eden
(seated, far left), and Roosevelt
(seated, second from left) meet in
Quebec, August 1943. Here Roosevelt
agreed to an invasion of Italy.

Several Hollywood heroes left the studios and served in the Forces, where the bullets were real and the good guys didn't always win. (*Above*) "Somewhere in England" Gunnery Instructor **Clark Gable** of the US Army Air Force smiles for the camera. (*Right*) Major **James Stewart** is decorated for heroic combat action in flying raids over Germany.

Showbiz stars and sporting celebrities went willingly to war, boosting morale at home and bringing a much needed touch of home to those serving overseas. (*Above*) **Joe Louis**, Heavyweight Champion of the World, signs autographs at Fort Devons. (*Right*) Comedienne **Martha Raye** stars in a USO-Camp Show in Constantine, Algeria.

The Stage Door canteen was a nightclub
for servicemen and women, run by the USO
in New York City. Its patrons often found
themselves facing the cream of Hollywood
when they reached the food counter. (*Above*)
Private Vazquez of gets a slice of cake from
Bette Davis, July 10, 1943.

The club inspired a 1943 movie with an all-star cast
that included Harpo Marx, Yehudi Menuhin, Katharine
Hepburn, "Tarzan", Gypsy Rose Lee, Benny Goodman
and his Orchestra, and the Count Basie Band.
(*Above*) A *March of Time* short called *Show Business
at War* was set in the equally famous Hollywood
canteen, and starred **Marlene Dietrich** (far right).

With the city cleared of German troops and
in the hands of the Allies, US soldiers march
past the monument to Victor Emmanuel II
in the Piazza Venezia, **Rome**, June 4, 1944.
Early that morning propaganda leaflets
dropped on the city urged: "Citizens of Rome,
this is not the time for demonstrations... Go
on with your regular work. Rome is yours!"

Troops of the US 5th Army entered Rome
in early June 1944. From that moment,
those who had collaborated with
Mussolini's Fascists or with the German
occupying army could expect
little mercy. (*Above*) Fellow citizens
threaten a **Fascist sympathizer** in Rome.

Pope Pius XII spoke from the balcony of
the Vatican Palace, rejoicing that "thanks
to the goodwill of both sides, Rome has
been saved from the horrors of war".
Goodwill was not to be found throughout
the Eternal City, however. (*Above*) **Revenge**
is extracted on another Fascist supporter.

(*Above*) US soldiers wade ashore early on D-Day, under intense fire from machine guns along the Normandy coast. (*Right*) Tracer fire from dozens of ships lights up the sky during the opening phase of the D-Day invasion.

1944   D-Day

Everyone knew that a massive Allied invasion of France was imminent. Few knew where it would take place – estimates varied from the Pas de Calais, right round the coast to the Pays Basque. Operation Overlord finally took place a day late, due to stormy weather. On June 6, 1944 at 06.00, two hours after Eisenhower had said "OK, let's go", the first US seaborne troops went ashore on the beaches of Normandy; the British followed one hour later. By the end of the day, 156,000 troops had landed, under heavy fire and with considerable losses, for German military command realized that their best chance of defeating the invasion was before it secured a bridgehead.

Further storms from June 19 to 22 slowed Allied progress. It took a week for the Americans to capture Cherbourg, while the British were bogged down around Caen. Eisenhower sent messages to the French people, asking them to be patient. On July 25, the Americans broke through, sweeping across northern France. Liberation had begun.

And still they come... (*Above*) A second wave of US troops
hits the beach on D-Day. Many landing craft were holed
by shells and sank fully loaded. Others were carried by
fierce tides more than two miles from their destination.

(*Above*) Troops of the Canadian 3rd Division arrive at Sword Beach, just to the west of Ouistreham. (*Below*) Wounded GIs are helped ashore after their landing craft sank near Utah Beach.

(*Left*) An aerial view of a Normandy beach on D-Day, taken when the beach had been secured and the fighting had moved a little further inland. One of the surprises of D-Day was the almost complete absence of the *Luftwaffe*. (*Above*) A day later, American infantrymen toast success at Sainte Mère Église.

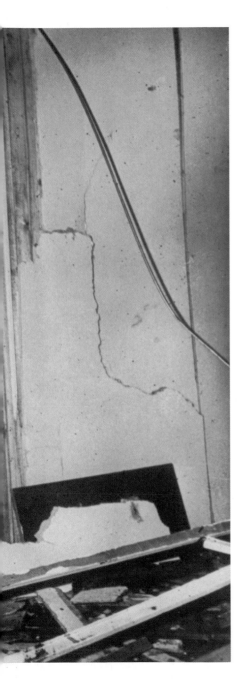

On July 22, 1944, Count von Stauffenberg placed
a **time bomb** in Hitler's command headquarters
at Rastenburg. The bomb exploded, but failed to
kill Hitler. (*Left*) Mussolini and Hitler inspect the
damage. In the fury of the aftermath, 200 people
were executed, among them Dr Carl Goerdeler,
Bürgermeister of Leipzig (seen above at his trial).

As Hitler's empire crumbled, armed resistance against Nazi occupation increased in all occupied countries. (*Above*) Members of the **French Resistance** take German prisoners following the liberation of Paris. (*Right*) A US Army officer and a French Resistance fighter pose for the camera on a Paris street.

Some did not live to see liberation. (*Above*)
Eight members of the *Francs-Tireurs et Partisans*
await **execution** by a German firing-squad in
Fort Mont Valerian, Paris, February 21, 1944.
The group included one Frenchman, three
Poles, one Hungarian, one Romanian, and their
Armenian-born leader Mussak Monouchian
(sixth from right). With liberation for the many
came retribution for the few. (*Right*) A young
French collaborator awaits execution.

In August 1944 Warsaw rose a second time against the Nazis. The Red Army was only nine miles (14 kilometers) away and the Polish Government in exile had urged the citizens of Warsaw to take up arms. (*Above*) Members of the **Polish Home Army**, some in captured German uniforms, bring up ammunition to the front line.

(*Above*) Soldiers of the Home Army with a captured German staff car. The rising lasted two months, but the Red Army, on Stalin's orders, made no attempt to come to the rescue of the Poles. Britain and the US also played a waiting game, with neither Churchill nor Roosevelt running the risk of offending their powerful Soviet ally. The end came with the **Polish surrender** on October 2. They had lost 200,000 men.

When the German Army withdrew from
Paris a few Nazi extremists stayed
behind to fight to the death. (*Left*)
Parisians take cover on the Pont d'Arcole
near the Hôtel de Ville, as a sniper fires
on them. (*Above*) Crowds cheer the arrival
of Allied tanks at the Arc de Triomphe.

On August 31, six days after the Allies marched into Paris, the first six members of the US **Women's Army Corps** entered the city. More followed: typists, telephonists, file clerks, drivers, and stenographers. They worked primarily in the Finance Office and the Post Exchange, but were also to be found in the fashion houses and perfume shops (*above*).

The honor of being the first army to march into Paris was given to the Free French under General Leclerc. Others followed soon after, and by September there were thousands of troops billeted in the city. (*Above*) British soldiers join their **Parisian hosts** in a toast to *La Liberation*.

A selection of photographer Bob Landry's **Paris fashion** studies, taken not long after liberation. With the exception of the railings (*above*), the pictures were all taken with relevant, if not suitable, military backgrounds and stage furnishings. Landry went on to play himself in the 1945 film *GI Joe*.

The **Greek Resistance** was composed of a variety of irregular groups know as *Andastes* (*above*). These units did not necessarily share the same political opinions or aspirations. Co-operation between them was limited and they were often poorly armed. (*Right*) Watched by partisans, a British paratrooper pins a Union Jack emblem on a boy's sleeve at Megara airfield, west of Athens, October 25, 1944.

Among the fiercest opponents of Nazi occupation were the **Yugoslav partisans** under their leader Josip Broz, better known by his codename Tito. (*Above*) Yugoslav partisans warily approach a German post at Litja, Slovenia, November 17, 1944. (*Right*) From his mountain headquarters, **Tito** communicates by field telephone with his officers in August 1944. His dog was a faithful companion throughout the war.

The film of *Henry V* was made in 1944, the intention being that its heroic theme would boost morale at home. It was partly funded by the British Government and was co-written, directed by and starred **Laurence Olivier**, who was paid £15,000 tax free for his work.

Catherine was Great opened in New York in the summer of 1944, starring **Mae West** (*above*) and produced by Mike Todd. The critics described it as a "fancy un-dress affair". In her first night curtain speech, Mae West said: "Catherine had 300 lovers in her life. I did the best I could in two hours".

The American President, Franklin D
Roosevelt, did not live to see the death of
his two arch-enemies, Hitler and Mussolini.
Already a very sick man when he met with
Churchill and Stalin at the **Yalta** Conference
(*above*) on February 11, 1945, he died two
weeks later. (*Right*) **Roosevelt's body** lies in
a casket draped with the Stars and Stripes.

When the war ended little compassion was
shown towards women who had **"fraternized"**
with German occupying forces. (*Above*) Members
of the Danish Resistance round-up women
guilty of this crime. (*Right*) Two French women
are publicly shamed by anti-Fascists. Inhabitants
of countries that had not been occupied in the
war found such images unacceptable.

With the liberation of Poland, Austria and later Germany came the discovery of the **concentration camps** and the horrors that had taken place within. (*Left*) A German SS officer and a female former camp guard place the bodies of victims in a mass grave. (*Right*) The bodies of some 3,000 slave laborers at the Nazi underground factory in Nordhausen are prepared for burial.

(*Left*) John Florea's photograph of an emaciated inmate of the **Nordhausen Camp**, taken shortly after the camp was liberated. Never before had such suffering and such cruelty been brought to the world's attention.

Prisoners at the **Gusen Camp** in Mauthausen, Austria were forced to work in nearby stone quarries until they were too weak to work. Then they were shot. (*Above*) Bodies of the victims, loaded on a cart by local citizens, await burial.

(*Above*) **East meets West** near Targan on the River Elbe, April 25, 1945, as Lieutenant William Robertson hugs Lieutenant Alexander Sylvashko of the 1st Ukrainian Army. Hitler's Reich had less than a week left.

As the German army retreated, it destroyed bridges over the major rivers. (*Above*) Refugees and displaced persons cross what is left of the **Elbe** bridge at Tangermünde. The photograph was one of many taken by Fred Ramage in the dying days of the European war.

For some time **Mussolini** and his mistress, Clara
Petacci, had been on the run. In the spring of 1945
they attempted to escape from Italy into Switzerland,
but on April 28 they were captured by Italian partisans,
summarily tried and executed. Their bullet-ridden
bodies (*right*) were then brought to Milan, and hung
upside down on public display (*above*).

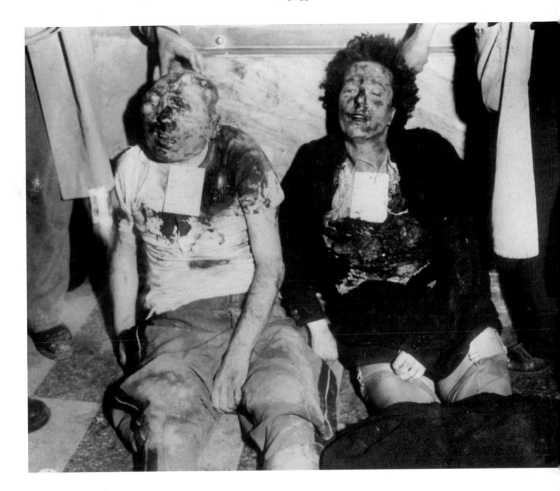

Allied bombing raids on German cities intensified as the war
neared its bitter end. One of the worst hit was **Cologne**, on which
the USAF dropped 50,000 tons of bombs. The *Dom* (*above*) was
gutted, though its nave and spires miraculously survived. (*Left*)
A German woman takes a break from her search for a new home.

Although the final collapse of Hitler's *Reich* was swift, the suffering of the German people was to be long and arduous. (*Above*) **Refugees** pick their way through Berlin streets in the early days of peace. (*Right*) Leonard McCombe's study of homeless Germans surviving in an abandoned municipal building.

News of Germany's unconditional surrender was broadcast on German radio at lunchtime on May 7, 1945. Across Europe those that survived almost six years of slaughter took to the streets in joy and relief. Many went to their place of worship to give thanks to God. Others wanted time alone, to meditate on what, and who they had lost. A few looked to the future, to the continuing war against Japan and beyond, wondering if politicians would keep the promises they had made about "a better world to come". When V-J Day came just over three months later the rejoicing was world wide for the victors. The defeated Japanese, reeling from the shock of Hiroshima and Nagasaki, heard the voice of their Emperor for the first time, in a broadcast that talked not of surrender but of "ceasefire". Some could not live with the shame and committed suicide. Others, in caves on Pacific islands, refused to accept it and fought on. But the guns were silent, and the planes that flew overhead no longer posed a threat.

(*Previous page – top left*) George
Broomhead of the Royal navy waves the
Union Jack, the Stars and Stripes, and
the Hammer and Sickle from the top of
one of the lions in Trafalgar Square, May 8,
1945: (right) Churchill acknowledges
crowds in Whitehall on the same day.

(*This page – left*) An impromptu party
on the Boulevard de Clichy, Paris on V-E
Day. (*Above*) A party in Tilloch Street,
London. (*Right*) Bill Eckert's impersonation
of Hitler attracts the attention of revelers
in Times Square, NYC.

(*Above*) American troops in Paris on V-J Day carry the Stars and Stripes and a banner that reads "JAPS LICKED". (*Below*) A Japanese POW in Bilibid Prison, Manila, gets news of the war's end from the *Daily Pacifican*.

"Let joy be unconfined..." (*Right*) Alfred Eisenstaedt's portrait of a sailor communicating something of what he feels to a nurse in uniform in the middle of Times Square, New York City on V-J Day.

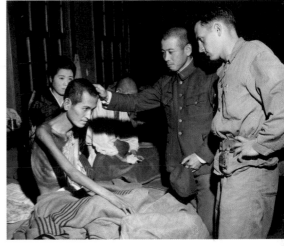

On Monday, August 6, 1945 at 09.15 the *Enola Gay*, a Super-Fortress piloted by Colonel Paul W Tibbets Junior, flew over the Japanese city of Hiroshima. The bomb it dropped had more power than 20,000 tons of TNT. The age of the **A-Bomb** was launched and 60,000 people were killed instantly. Many more died subsequently. (*Left*) Devastation at Hiroshima. (*Above*) A victim of the second A-Bomb, dropped on Nagasaki, is examined by Dr Shigeru Kawada and US Navy Lieutenant Thomas Brown (right).

Following the destruction of Hiroshima and Nagasaki, **Japan surrendered** to the Allies on board *USS Missouri* in Tokyo Bay. General Douglas MacArthur (standing behind the chair) accepted the surrender in front of representatives of the Allied nations. (*Left*) The crew of the *USS Missouri* looks on as the Japanese delegation faces MacArthur and his officers.

Whatever side you were on, a **soldier's return** was a blessed and poignant moment. (*Left*) A German POW, released in the summer of 1945, receives a warm welcome home. (*Right*) A loved one is swept off her feet by a returning GI in the aptly named town of New Hope, Pennsylvania.

Stars of "stage, screen, and radio" visited the troops in their training camps and followed them across mainland Europe after the D-Day landings. (*Left*) **Marlene Dietrich** holds servicemen spellbound as she reads from a notebook at Camp Meade, Vermont. (*Above*) The comedian **Bob Hope** takes his time while signing an autograph for a member of the Motor Transport Corps outside the Savoy Theatre, London.

Money spent by the public on entertainment more than doubled during the war. The greatest beneficiary was the film industry. The studio system was at its height, the stars at their most dazzling, among them **Bogart and Bacall** (*above*), seen here rehearsing on the set of *The Big Sleep*. Hollywood continued to attract much talent from Europe. (*Right*) Director **Jean Renoir** prepares to shoot a scene for *The Southerner*.

Acute and chronic shortages of food, fuel, and luxury items continued long after the war ended. Rationing remained, but there was always the **Black Market** for those with money or something to trade. (*Left*) A Canadian airman sells lighters in Cutler Street, London. (*Right*) Women in Rome offer home-baked bread for sale.

The war also created hundreds of thousands of orphaned and **homeless children,** many of whom had simply become detached from their parents as refugees struggled across Europe. (*Right*) Cardinal Theodor Innitzer – perhaps unkindly labeled the "Heil Hitler Cardinal" – attends a party for such children in Austria.

Life was a battle, a primitive existence for many, often without home, job, or money. In the worst hit areas, **scavenging** became the daily means of existence. (*Above*) Women in post-war Berlin search for cigarette butts and kitchen scraps amongst the trash and rubble outside a British barracks.

There was so much to be done. Life at a very basic level had to be rebuilt across much of the world. (*Left*) Former President **Herbert Hoover**, Chairman of the Famine Emergency Committee, visits a camp for displaced Polish children.

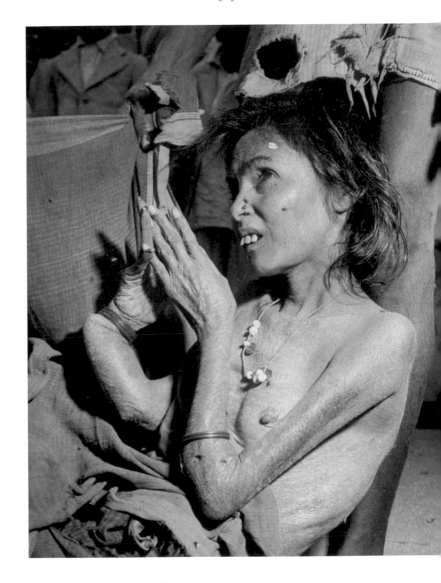

For some, the rebuilding of life was not possible. In the grip of a **famine in India**, a deformed woman lies in a sling made from a sari. Government workers had carried her to a relief kitchen.

The collapse of the Japanese Empire in the
East created chaos in parts of **China**. Chiang Kai
Shek attempted to maintain power in cities
along China's eastern seaboard; elsewhere the
Communists were in command. (*Above*) Japanese
laborers restore Red Square, Mukden.

The USSR withdrew its troops from **China**, although many signs of its wartime presence remained. (*Above*) A shopkeeper waits for customers in Mukden. Behind him is a portrait of Josef Stalin and a poster celebrating the alliance between the USSR and China.

Dr Marcel Petiot had claimed that he could help Jews escape from Paris during the Nazi occupation. After taking their money, Petiot killed them in his home-made gas chamber in his cellar. Brought to trial after the war, he was convicted of 24 murders. (*Above*) Petiot in the dock, March 19, 1946. (*Left*) The luggage of his victims, found by police at Petiot's house.

In the long wait for the creation of the state of Israel, fighting broke out in Palestine, where the Stern Gang and others used violence to speed the British departure. (*Left*) A woman – probably a hotel worker – is taken for **questioning** by British troops. (*Right*) Soldiers search for survivors of the **King David Hotel bombing** in Jerusalem, July 22, 1946.

The establishment of the long-promised land took too long for many Jews, who anticipated the event by seeking to enter Palestine clandestinely. (*Above*) **Jewish immigrants** await the day in the Caraolos internment camp, Cyprus. (*Right*) Some of the 4,000 Jews who were living on ships in Haifa Harbor, August 1946.

The trials of those Nazis accused of war crimes began at **Nuremberg** on November 20, 1945 and lasted well over a year. (*Above*) A mass trial in October 1946 – among the accused are (left to right, sitting in front row) Hermann Goering, Rudolf Hess, Joachim von Ribbentrop, and Wilhelm Keitel.

Of the 12 war criminals sentenced to death, Martin Bormann was sentenced *in absentia*, and Goering took his own life. The sentencing of two senior *Wehrmacht* officers – Keitel and Alfred Jodl – caused controversy. They claimed they were following the orders of their supreme commander, Adolf Hitler, and then demanded death by firing squad rather than hanging. (*Above*) The body of **Alfred Jodl**, October 16, 1946.

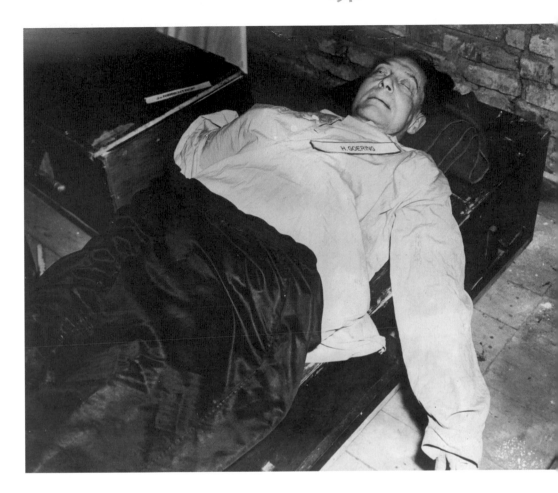

At Nuremberg, Goering's defense lawyer
was Dr Otto Stahmer (*left*, with his back to
camera). **Goering** chose to conduct much of
his own defense, however, declaring that he
had never been anti-Semitic. The night
before he was to be executed, he swallowed
a capsule of potassium cyanide that had
somehow been smuggled in to him.

Free from the morale boosting demands of
government, the European film industry showed
signs of recovery in 1946. (*Above* – left to right)
Jean Marais, Jean Cocteau, Josette Day, and Michel
Auclair discuss filming on the set of Cocteau's
La Belle et La Bête. (*Right*) F J McCormick (on
right) leads a wounded James Mason through the
streets of Belfast in Carol Reed's **Odd Man Out**.

The nationalist movement for Indian independence had grown considerably during the war. The Raj had lost much of its prestige following the ease with which Japanese troops had initially defeated the British army. Nevertheless, immense obstacles stood in the way of a transfer of power. Churchill was passionately opposed to Indian independence, and there was the problem of how the sub-continent might be divided to preserve the safety and freedom of worship for Hindus, Muslims, Sikhs, and others.

The establishment of Attlee's Labour Government in 1945 paved the way for change. A new Viceroy was appointed – Lord Louis Mountbatten – who had the courage to pluck a date from the air and announce that, from that day, India would no longer be the Jewel in the British Crown. The date fixed for independence was August 15, 1947.

Slaughter preceded freedom for both India and Pakistan, with riots in the major cities. (*Above*) Fighting on the streets of Bombay. (*Below*) British troops patrol Calcutta, following armed clashes between Hindus and Muslims. (*Right*) Vultures line the rooftops while bodies of both sides lie in the Calcutta streets.

The eventual handover of power was perhaps the best planned operation in 200 years of British rule. (*Above*) British Cabinet Commission members Frederick Pethick-Lawrence (left) and Sir Stafford Cripps (right) in conference with Mohammed Ali Jinnah, May 1946. (*Left*) Hindu leader Jawaharial Nehru. (*Right*) The last Viceroy – Mountbatten – with Mahatma Gandhi (center) and Lady Edwina Mountbatten.

As Independence Day approached, millions of people journeyed across the sub-continent to new homes. (*Above*) Muslim women leave Delhi for the new state of Pakistan. (*Left*) Sikhs head for East Punjab. (*Right*) Crowds celebrate independence in Calcutta.

The first quarter of 1947 brought Arctic
weather conditions to a continent still
suffering from acute fuel shortages.
Countries unused to heavy and
prolonged snow had to adapt to survive.
(*Above*) **A milkman in Cheam**, near
London, abandons his horse and cart.

Snow piled up even in city centers. (*Above*) **A policeman on traffic duty** near St Paul's Cathedral, London, is allowed the luxury of a small mat to prevent his feet freezing.

Months passed and the snow
continued. (*Above*) Somewhere north
of London, en route to the Boat Race,
the **Cambridge University boat race
crew** attempt to rescue their bus from
a snow drift, April 10, 1947. They won.

Soldiers, civilians, and prisoners-of-war were detailed to snow-clearing duties. (*Above*) **German POWs** reclaim a road near Chapel-en-le-Frith, England, after yet another blizzard, February 6, 1947.

E 2

And still the state of Israel had not been created... (*Above*) The famous immigration ship **Exodus** waits in Haifa, July 18, 1947. (*Left*) A study by Erich Auerbach of Jewish refugees making their forbidden journey to Palestine.

The Paris fashion houses continued to make their stylish cuts during the war. (*Left*) A Jacques Fath model poses beside a 1947 **Delahaye coupe**. (*Right*) Fashion photographer **Louise Dahl-Wolfe** takes a shot for *Harpers' Bazaar*.

The **House Un-American Activities Committee** (HUAC) was formed in 1938. In 1947 it turned its attention to Hollywood, seeking to rid Tinseltown of any Red Menace. (*Left*) "Friendly" witnesses included (clockwise from top left) Gary Cooper, Robert Taylor, and Jack L Warner. Bertholt Brecht, with cigar, claimed he was not a member of the Communist Party. (*Above*) Those "warned off" included (left to right, standing) Danny Kaye, June Havoc, and Humphrey Bogart.

(*Left*) **Howard Hughes** surveys the inside of the fuselage of his H-4 Hercules flying boat. The body of the giant aircraft was built of laminated birch, not spruce as its nickname *Spruce Goose* suggested. It flew only once, in 1947, when it was airborne for just one mile.

(*Above*) **Major Charles E Yeager** – *aka* Mr Supersonic, The Fastest Guy Alive and "the guy with the right stuff" – holds a model of the Bell-X1 rocket research plane. On October 14, 1947, he became the first pilot to break the sound barrier.

For the British public, a beacon of romance and glamour shining in the dark postwar days was the **wedding of Princess Elizabeth** to Philip Mountbatten, nephew of the ex-Viceroy of India. After leaving Westminster Abbey at the end of the ceremony (*left*), the couple drove to Buckingham Palace and (*above*) acknowledged the cheers of the crowd below, November 20, 1947. (*Right*) Mr Schur (second from left) and colleagues inspect the official wedding cake, baked in the ovens of Huntley and palmer. It was nine feet (2.7 meters) high.

(*Above*) **Jackie Robinson** goes for a
double play. Robinson was the first African
American to play major league baseball.
(*Right*) **Joe Louis** is knocked down by
Jersey Joe Walcott at Madison Square
Garden, December 1947. Louis recovered
to retain his World Heavyweight title.

On January 30, 1948, **Mahatma Gandhi** was shot by Nathuram Godse, a member of an extreme Hindu sect. (*Above*) Gandhi's body lies in state at Birla House, New Delhi. (*Left*) The funeral pyre of the world's most famous advocate of non-violence. (*Right*) Crowds watch Gandhi's funeral.

In February 1948 a Communist
coup led to a new regime,
a "government of the
workers", in Czechoslovakia.
(*Left*) The new Premier,
Klement Gottwald, addresses
crowds from the Kinsky Palace
in Old City Square, Prague.
France, Britain, and the United
States protested, but
Gottwald replied: "We will
never take lessons in
democracy from those with
Munich on their conscience."

The **new state of Israel** finally
came into being on May 14,
1948. (*Above*) As first Prime
Minister, David Ben-Gurion
stands to read the Proclamation
of Nationhood. (*Right*) Young
Jewish citizens take to the
streets of Tel Aviv to celebrate
the glorious day.

In June 1948, an ex-troopship, the *Empire Windrush* (*right*), sailed into Tilbury Docks, London. On board were 482 **Jamaican immigrants**, seeking work in the Mother Country. (*Above*) A temporary hostel for the new arrivals in an old air-raid shelter beneath Clapham Common, London.

The Soviet Union's **blockade of Berlin** began in June 1948,
cutting off the city from the rest of Western Germany.
For almost a year, a round-the-clock "air lift" kept the city
going and its inhabitants alive. (*Above*) Sacks of flour
arrive at Tempelhof Airport. (*Right*) Children in a tree near
the Brandenburg Gate watch yet another US cargo plane.

(*Above*) H S Bignall (right) lights a new torch for the Olympic Flame in Reigate, Surrey, July 28, 1948. Thirty miles (48 kilometers) ahead lay Wembley.
(*Left*) Officials and athletes process towards the Stadium for the opening ceremony the following day.

Germany and Japan were banned from the 1948 Olympic Games, which were held in London as no other city either wished or could afford to act as host. Over 4,000 competitors from 59 nations attended, accepting in good spirit the at times humble accommodation offered in schools and former Army or POW camps. Only the Press complained. The weather was glorious (save for one day) and Sigfrid Edstrom, President of the International Olympic Commission praised his hosts: "It was", he said, "a challenge to the British genius for improvisation, and the organization rose gloriously to the supreme challenge".

Emil Zatopek takes gold in the 10,000 Meters. (*Right*) Gaston Reiff of Belgium with supporter after winning the 5,000 Meters gold medal in pouring rain.

(*Left*) The Flying Dutchwoman, Fanny Blankers-Koen, takes the lead in the 80 Meter Hurdles. It was one of the four gold medals she won in the Games. (*Above*) R M Stigersand of Norway competes in the Men's Platform Diving competition at the Empire Pool, Wembley. At least one diver mistook the panes of glass in the ceiling for the lanes in the water, and belly-flopped.

223

In the late 1940s, Paris was the center of the literary and philosophical world, a city where the Old Guard and the *avant-garde* gathered together. (*Above*) **Suzanne Beliot**, **Jean Cocteau** (centre) and **Jean-Paul Sartre** at a rehearsal of Sartre's *Les Mains Sales*. (*Left*) A portrait by Lipnitzki of the French writer **Colette**, May 1948. (*Right*) **André Gide** (with rug), **Madeleine Renaud**, and her husband **Jean-Louis Barrault**.

Still in self-imposed exile from Franco's Spain, **Pablo Picasso** (*left*) sits beside a recent sculpture in his studio at Vallauris, France. (*Right*) A portrait of the Swiss painter and sculptor **Alberto Giacometti**. When the war ended, he left Geneva to return to Paris.

Two American modernists. (*Left*) Painter and sculptor
Alexander Calder assembles one of his works for
an exhibition in a New York gallery, January 1948.
(*Above*) **Jackson Pollock** drips paint – and ash – on
a new canvas. A year earlier he had developed his
"pour" technique, the brush never touching the canvas.

The book that shook the world... (*Left*) **Professor Alfred Kinsey**, zoologist, biologist, and student of human behavior. In 1947 he had founded the Institute for Research in Sex, Gender and Reproduction.

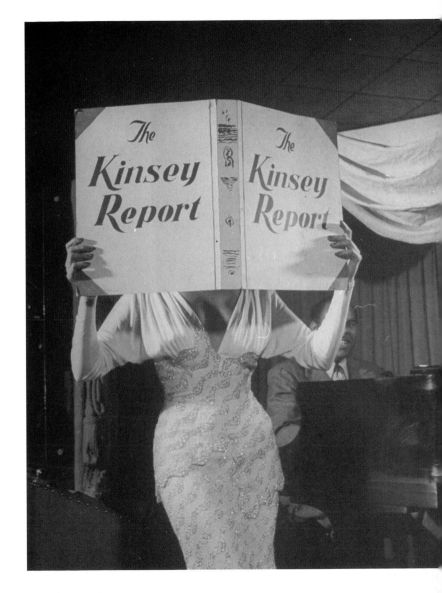

The Kinsey Report into the Sexual Behavior of the Human Male was published in 1948, to the delight of comedians and cabaret stars. (*Above*) Julie Wilson sings her way through *The Kinsey Report* at the Mocambo Club, Hollywood.

In the late 1940s, the Cold War
escalated in the Far East as
the failing British Empire
neared its last gasp. (*Above*)
Burmese Government troops
receive their orders for an
attack on Communist guerrillas.

One of the most protracted imperial campaigns was fought in **Malaya,** where British rubber planters feared that every native Malayan might be a Communist agent. (*Above*) Police patrol a railway line through the Malayan jungle.

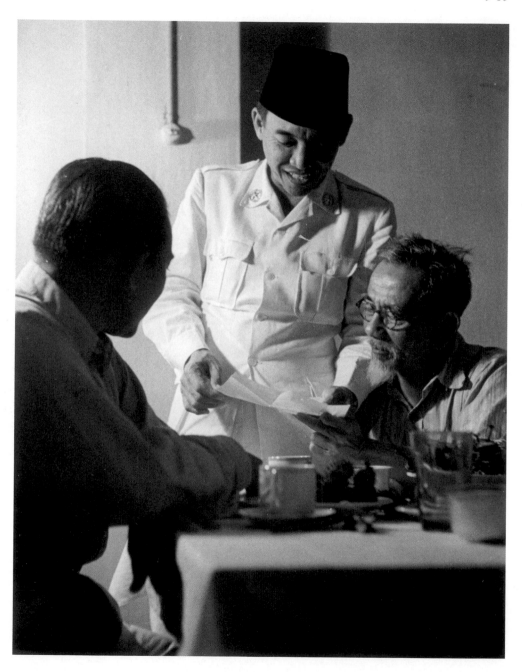

(Left) Indonesian President **Achmed Sukarno** (center) and his Foreign Minister Haji Salim (right) discuss papers. They had been released from prison, but still awaited Indonesian independence in April 1949.

Britain was not the only colonial power in the Far East that had to swallow its pride. (Above) Queen Juliana of the Netherlands (center) watches her Prime Minister, William Drees, sign the document granting **Indonesian independence**, December 27, 1949.

Under pressure from the US, the Dutch began
evacuating troops from Indonesia in the
summer of 1949. (*Above*) US Marines approach
the **oil center at Tjepoe**, Eastern Java. The
smoke comes from fires started by Republican
forces as part of a scorched-earth policy.

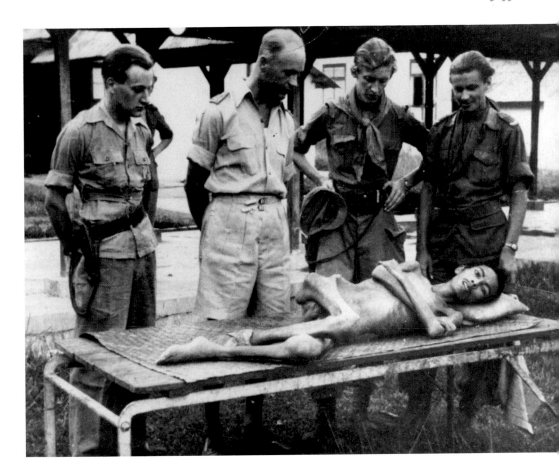

(*Above*) An Indonesian victim of the War of Independence is peremptorily examined by three Dutch soldiers and a doctor (second from left) outside a **Dutch military hospital** in northern Sumatra.

By the autumn of 1949, the civil war in China was virtually over. (*Left*) Communist troops advance on the city of Shanghai, May 21, 1949. (*Right*) Mao Tse-Tung proclaims the creation of the **People's Republic of China** in Beijing, October 1949. (*Above*) Communist troops of the East River Unit celebrate their arrival on the border with Hong Kong, October 25, 1949.

The Federal Republic of Germany was proclaimed on May 23, 1949, formalizing the split between East and West. Popular opinion saw Germany now as a land of two political philosophies and two cultures. (*Above*) **Police in the Eastern Sector** of Berlin march through the streets on a May Day rally.

(*Right*) The trademark of the West... **Volkswagen "Beetles"** await buyers on a factory parking lot. The People's Car did much to promote postwar belief in German industrial reliability.

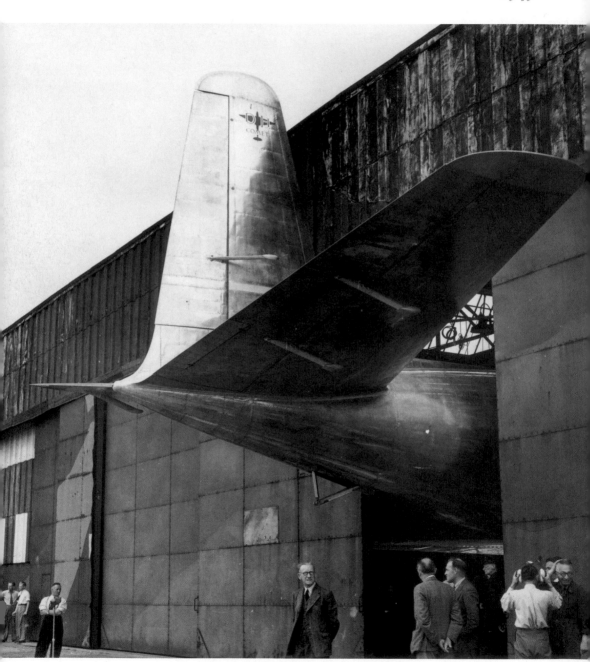

The **De Haviland Comet** (*above*) was the first jet-powered passenger airplane. It made its maiden flight on July 27, 1949, although its unorthodox emergence from the hangar on that day (*left*) may have occasioned some surprise.

It was the dawn of the great age of gas-guzzling, chrome-laden, broad-chassised American limos, luxuriously transporting the ideal family down the highways of freedom. (*Above*) A **Ford convertible** of 1949, complete with glamorous model.

Europe looked for more economical means of road transport – the 2CV, the Morris Minor, the Volkswagen Beetle, and (*right*) a prototype **French folding car**, its owner evincing Tati-esque delight.

The new wonder of the age was television, a pre-war invention but one that only began to make its mark on everyday life-style in the late 1940s. (*Above*) The world's **first commercial color-TV** goes into action at the National Radio Exhibition, Olympia, London September 28, 1949.

At the same show, visitors could admire the
smooth contours and discreet control panel of the
Dynatron "Sovereign", a 34-valve, 12-inch screen
combined radio, gramophone, and TV set.
It cost six month's salary for the average worker.

Fashion hit sports in the shape of **"Gorgeous" Gussie Moran**, an American tennis player. (*Above*) On June 20, 1949 she appeared on Wimbledon's Center Court in a "shocking" outfit designed by Teddy Tinling. (*Right*) Open Champion **Bobby Locke** preferred a more conservative outfit for the Harrogate Golf Tournament that year.

American playwrights brought new life and new realism to the theater with plays by Clifford Odets, William Inge, Arthur Miller, and Tennessee Williams. (*Above*) Elia Kazan (left) and Miller on the Broadway set of **Death of a Salesman**. (*Right*) Bonar Colleano and Vivien Leigh do battle in a performance of **A Streetcar Named Desire** at the Aldwych Theatre, London, October 22, 1949.

The cinema also broke new ground. The old Broadway backstage musicals of Busby Berkeley and others were replaced by MGM's almost revolutionary **On the Town**, directed by Gene Kelly and Stanley Donen, and with a score by Leonard Bernstein. (*Above*) Kelly and Vera Ellen in the dream ballet sequence from the film.

One idea that got off the
ground, but not for long, was
the **Fly-In Movie Theater**,
which catered for helicopters
and small piston engine
planes. (*Above*) Such novelties
did still cater for their drive-in
customers, however.

One of the finest European films of 1949 was
The Third Man, which starred Orson Welles
(*right*) as the fugitive Harry Lime. It was located
and shot in Vienna and also starred Joseph
Cotton (*above* – looking over the shoulder of
director Carol Reed). The film won an Oscar for
its Director of Photography, Robert Krasker.

Index
Page numbers refer to text references